OOOHH PINTERESTING!

HOW TO USE PINTEREST TO CONVERT CLIENTS AND GET MORE WEBSITE TRAFFIC

ALLY DAVIS

authors
AND CO.

CONTENTS

ABOUT THE AUTHOR

Hey, I'm Ally - a lover of Pinterest, creative content and photography. I'm known for leading with my heart and helping women bring their brand and presence to life online. You'll usually find me at home in Wales, drinking tea with my Labrador puppy Freddie and redesigning our home!

My story is one of finding strength, hope and honesty. Through my personal journey I managed to join my passion and skill for being creative with a determination to help others succeed.

I have invested lots of time in learning the techniques and processes needed to ensure I can support people and that they get the results they deserve. I have designed a business where I can help other females bring their brand online and be supported in doing so.

I believe Pinterest is a game changer and I hope this book will help you to see how and why you should be using Pinterest for your business. Not only that, but also how you can start converting traffic into results.

While everyone else is talking about Facebook and Instagram, I want you to be reaping the rewards of Pinterest and with a few hopefully easy steps you can start seeing the benefits.

Pinterest isn't a social media platform, it's a search engine where your ideal clients are hanging out. You need to be using Pinterest as it's an integral part of your marketing strategy - it can help you build an email list, boost traffic to your website and ultimately sell your business, service or product!

I hope you enjoy reading my book and sharing my love of Pinterest!

X

WHY PINTEREST?

"A YEAR FROM NOW YOU MAY WISH YOU HAD STARTED TODAY"

Starting a business in Pinterest wasn't on my radar. I knew I wanted to work for myself and that a typical office environment wasn't where I thrived. After a conversation with my business coaches two years ago they suggested I look into creating a business around Pinterest.

I had used Pinterest for several years for my own inspiration and collections but never thought about focussing a business around it.

Pinterest is such an inspirational platform. It's designed to motivate and plan out your moments. I use it for any research I need to do as I find the images resonate with me rather than a list. I have spent the last two years researching everything there is to know about Pinterest, taking various courses and working on different accounts for experience. I find Pinterest is so inspirational and it represents everything, so why wouldn't I create my business around it?

This book is designed to show you the benefits of Pinterest, why you should be using it and how to use it. Pinterest is a traffic referral platform and I want to help show you how you can create more traffic and conversions by using it.

Using this process does not need to increase your time using the platform, but instead use it more strategically.

I do hope this book becomes a well-worn useful guide for you and if you want to learn more about my life and business check out my Pinterest and Instagram accounts or alternatively my website for further tips, blogs and articles.

WHAT IS PINTEREST?

"PINTEREST IS A VISUAL SEARCH ENGINE"

Ok, so feel free to skip over this chapter if you are a Pinterest Guru already (pinning and re-pinning daily with lots of beautiful boards) but I want to start at the beginning. What is Pinterest?

Pinterest was first designed in 2009 with the first prototype in 2010. It has developed into a very successful site being funded by investors and entrepreneurs and in 2017 the company was valued at €12 billion. Retail companies use Pinterest for design, styling and advertising.

Pinterest is a search engine, just like Google, and all the others but it uses visual discovery instead. A lot of people think that Pinterest is a social media platform, but it is not. If you are yet to use Pinterest (um, hello get on there!) it is made up of images, graphics and videos and when a search is completed you are given image results. These images could be just a photo or a product advert, something to buy or information represented by images.

It allows people to discover and share new images and it's full of people looking to buy items, shop for clothes, purchase self-development or read blog posts and articles. You may or may not be surprised to learn that all types of genres are on this platform. I challenge you to think of something really niche or obscure and see if it's there - I have found all sorts on there from religious studies to dating to self-development!

Pinterest is also used as a problem solver. People will search for an answer to their question or just for a new recipe for tonight's dinner - the options really are endless! If you are using Pinterest already I am sure you are probably using it for tonight's dinner recipe, your dream interior and your bucket list!

You will find everything from articles, blog posts, products, photography, courses, education and recipes. At the time of writing this book Pinterest has over 200 million users!

There are over 50 billion pins (that number blows my mind!) - I don't think however long I am addicted to Pinterest I will ever get through them all! Have a look at your favourite hobby or business and complete a search. What did you find? Was it something you could use now or in the future?

Let's take the example that you want a new pair of shoes - you have the colour, style, type all planned out - why not search for this in Pinterest? I'm sure you already use Google or your favourite search engine to search.

There are over 2 million shopping pins that are saved daily and Pinterest helps people decide what they buy offline as well as online. Your search results will consist of adverts, shop links and Instagram pictures as well as Pinterest user's photographs for inspiration.

Pinterest is just like a traditional search engine, except your search results are images. You can purchase right from an image on Pinterest.

It's also great for story boards, creating mood and inspiration boards and works really well if working with clients for things such as brand shoots, shopping experiences etc. It has a whole host of genres, products and services just like Google or any search engine.

WHO IS PINTEREST FOR?

So you might be reading this thinking "so it's just for women and another way of shopping"! Well actually yes, the majority of users are women but Pinterest is actually for anyone.

It isn't just a shopping source. It is a great way of finding new books to read, podcasts to listen to, educational material and also for finding local business owners. Year on year more men are signing up so it represents all genders.

There are fantastic articles to read and a huge number of bloggers too. And you know how I said Pinterest isn't a social media platform? Well, it is social if you want to be! You can network, find local businesses and influencers that you want to work with or follow.

You can also find boards and pins that are local to you - local coffee shops, local artists to visit and so on. You can join groups and follow people of interest, make comments and try out pins but remember as it's not a social media platform you don't have to be social if you don't want to!

HOW DOES IT WORK?

Pinterest works on an algorithm to make a smart feed. But don't panic - it's not like Facebook or Instagram! It's a lot less complicated and far friendlier! Any content you share or pin can be seen by anyone. If someone follows you they will automatically see your content in their feed and get notified when you pin.

But even people that don't follow you will find your content in their search results and news feed. Pinterest is about quality not quantity and creating good content that people are searching for. The algorithm works for you not against you, getting your content in front of the right people.

When searching for a topic, you will receive your search results and rather than being listed in chronological order they will be listed based on pinner quality (based on the quality of your own uploaded pins), image quality, relevance and content quality - this makes the smart feed.

Now I know that sounds complicated but it really isn't.

If you are contributing to Pinterest you just need to ensure you are adding good quality pins - more on that later.

Pinterest wants to make the experience for the user, and the content the user sees, relevant so it uses the smart feed to score the pins and ensure that when you (the user) completes a search the results are what you are looking for.

Try it out – have a go at completing some searches and seeing what results you get and if you aren't on Pinterest get signed up!

THE STATS!

Pinterest has over 290 million active users across the world! They are logging in, using it to search for seasonal trends, daily inspiration and holiday planning. Every day Pinterest helps people discover, plan and buy.

More than 50% of users are now located outside of the US and there are over 4 billion boards! In the UK, 1 in 2 people are millennials and use Pinterest to influence their decision when shopping.

83% of women on Pinterest use it to plan their life moments and be inspired to create a life they love. This compares to 44% for Instagram and 53% for Facebook.

Did you know that brand marketers use Pinterest as an active part of their marketing strategy? 27% of marketers use Pinterest now and you will see videos and branded adverts from brands such as Asda, Next, TK Maxx, IKEA, eBay and so on.

Pinterest comes in a handy little app so more than 80% use it on their mobile. Whilst out and about, commuting and travelling you can search for inspiration, follow brands and find things that are relevant.

People come to Pinterest with a shopping mindset, open to discovering products to buy. Pinterest has over 175 billion pins that have been saved by others and are tried and tested so they can show you what is trending and best for you.

So if this doesn't urge you to get on there I don't know what will. You really are missing out on traffic and buyers if you don't use Pinterest.

Chapter Key Thoughts

- It's a search engine not social media
- Just like Google except uses images
- Pinterest is for pretty much anyone
- Your content gets seen by everyone not just those who follow you
- Over 250 million active users!
- People use Pinterest to be inspired, plan and buy

HOW TO NAVIGATE PINTEREST

"WHEN YOU FEEL LIKE QUITTING THINK ABOUT WHY YOU STARTED"

I'm going to go through how you navigate Pinterest now! It's difficult to write down the technical elements so if you are having any trouble please go to my website (www.allydavis.com) for my free resources and tutorials.

PROFILE

Ensure you have written your bio including keywords. Ask yourself who do you help and what do you help them with?

Add a photo of your face or logo if the company isn't named after you (a photo tends to work better so use this if you can over a logo). The bio is only a short description of who you are so make sure it is concise and to the point. If you have a lead magnet (a webpage that appears in response to clicking on a graphic or image) or free resource be sure to add the link in.

SET UP YOUR BUSINESS ACCOUNT

Ensure you have set up your business account, rather than a personal account. A business account will give you added extras such as analytics and you will be able to verify your website in the settings.

Even if you aren't a business I recommend setting up a business account as it gives you more functionality and uses than just a personal account. If you have a personal account it is easy to transfer to a business account.

BRAND

As discussed earlier take time to identify your brand then adding it to your Pinterest. Even other people's content that you share needs to fit with your brand and be of value to your audience.

When your audience visits your Pinterest or sees your pin in the feed they need to instantly know it is yours!

Use Canva (a free graphic design platform) to easily make sure you are on brand!

CONSISTENCY

Be consistent! Pinterest will reward you if you pin every day rather than a lot of pins on one day of the week. You will show up in the audience's searches as well as be on the feed.

To keep your reach and engagement, you will see better results if you are pinning consistently. Also be consistent with your brand, look and colour scheme. You will attract your audience if your pins are clear, consistent and good quality. Try using the same typography to ensure you get that familiar feel.

Each small thing you do today will accumulate over time. The changes you make to your profile or pins will add up to become big effects in the long term. Stick with it and track any edits or changes you make as the results won't be instant.

COLLABORATION OVER COMPETITION – IT AIN'T ALL ABOUT YOU!

As I said Pinterest allows us to share and save other people's content. You will be rewarded for doing this as it will widen your network. People engage better if it's not just about you and the person whose content you've shared will be notified so you could build engagement there. You will also find your daily and monthly averages increase if you share other's content too.

When sharing other people's content make sure it is relevant to you or your business. If you want to save a recipe for dinner but your business is nothing about food save it to a secret board so you will be able to find it again but it won't confuse your audience.

FUN

Pinterest is fun! You are meant to be addicted like me! Don't get too hung up on all the ins and outs. Enjoy the process of seeing what works and what doesn't, engage with others, find content you like and have fun!

PINS – WHAT ARE THEY AND HOW DO THEY WORK?

There are several ways in which people can discover your content. People can pin your content. A Pin is an image or video that people add to Pinterest. People add Pins directly from websites or apps using the Save button. Any Pin can be saved and all Pins link back to their sources, which is how you can get referral traffic e.g. they could pin directly from Instagram or your website.

An average pin has about 1-3 months life span but it will stay on Pinterest forever so in theory it could be used time and time again. If you are ever stuck for content to create or words to use, use the Search Tool as this gives you an accurate representation of what people are searching.

Pins are organised by interest. People organise Pins into collections (called boards) and share their boards with others. The same Pin might be added to lots of different boards across lots of interests, making boards a great place to discover new ideas or inspiration.

Feeds are used to discover Pins. People can follow all of someone's boards or just the ones they like best. As they discover and follow more people and boards, their feed becomes more relevant and personal to their interests.

Make sure you enter the Pin description and use keywords explaining what the pin is about and how it can help them. You can also use hashtags in the description as some people search using these instead. But hashtags aren't as popular or valuable on Pinterest as they are on say Instagram so don't use too many.

It is not what you shout out to the world that determines your life....

It is what you whisper to yourself that has the most power

~Abigail Horne~

www.femalesuccessnetwork.com

Pin from Female Success Network

BOARDS

Boards are the collections in which you keep your pins. For example you could have an interior design board, an inspiration quote board etc. Start *out with 10, you can always add* more as the seasons change.

. . .

Brain storm 10 boards below.

When naming your boards - keep it simple. Think of keywords that your ideal audience will be searching for and try and focus your board around them. Your boards need to represent you, your brand and your business.

But DON'T FORGET they also need to reflect the INTERESTS OF YOUR AUDIENCE. Think about topics and how you're categorising them. Make sure that the description is relevant to your audience and isn't confusing.

VIDEO

You will hear a lot of platforms and bloggers talk about how video is now a best practice. And it is the same for Pinterest. You don't see a lot of videos on Pinterest but that's how you will stand out.

When you create a video for Pinterest it should be high resolution even if it's a small video; if the video is poor quality your audience won't click on it. Most videos will auto-play on mobile devices but may play without sound so you need to be able to convey your message without relying upon sound. Use subtitles or text overlay to help with this.

Keep your video short and choose an attractive cover image. As with all of your pins you want your audience to click on it. Ensure you are using clear descriptions and titles to help your video be discovered.

Lastly make your video informative or actionable. The

best rated videos are the ones where they show you how to do something or inspire you to try something new.

Chapter Key Thoughts

- Have fun!
- Be consistent with your boards and pins
- Ensure you set up a business account
- Keep in mind your audience and ensuring your descriptions aren't confusing
- Use video if you can

WHY USE PINTEREST?

"PINTEREST WILL INCREASE YOUR WEBSITE TRAFFIC"

Whether or not you have a business, Pinterest is a great tool to gain inspiration. You can save pins to a board of your choice to refer back to anytime at a later date. So in essence it's like making lots of mood boards.

You know when your Mum used to bring home the newest Argos catalogue and you would cut out and stick all your favourite toys and clothes on to paper (No... just me?!)

Well Pinterest is like this, just a far easier, less sticky and hassle-free way of storing all your ideas and inspiration in one place.

But a warning - it's addictive!

"I am a pin addict!"

I love going on the app and searching for new ideas, trends or something to learn. It's super inspirational and a great way to network and connect with others in your field. You can find everything and anything on there and I really find it helps me get my creativity flowing whether its for business or personal use.

Ok so let's take a different example that you are renovating your house and want ideas on how to decorate or style your house - everything from paint colours to interior design ideas. You can complete a search on Pinterest and what you will find is endless beautiful pictures that you can save on to your boards for inspiration but also for purchasing at a later date.

I am renovating my home at the moment and have been gathering ideas for months, from the current on-trend colour schemes, to baths I like and so on. It really is that easy and the point being that as the seller of the bath I want, you know it's likely that I will be back to click on that pin to purchase from you!

Most people are on the app with a shopping mindset so if you have something you sell it should be on Pinterest to inspire others.

So with that in mind, brainstorm your business - what images, pins, links and ideas could you be sharing on Pinterest?

PinTip: Pinterest is a great tool for inspiration so your ideal account to follow will be on there. It's not just for businesses.

Chapter Key Thoughts

- Pinterest is inspirational
- Just like a mood board – you can save lots of ideas to come back to later
- It's addictive!

WHY USE PINTEREST FOR BUSINESS?

"PINTEREST IS AN OPPORTUNITY FOR YOU TO SHOWCASE YOUR BUSINESS"

Ok, ok I know you are probably thinking I barely have time to keep up with my social media let alone invest time in to learning a new platform. Or you may already be an excellent pinner and can't see how what I've got to say will help your business.

Firstly let's go over what you have already read - yes, I use Pinterest for nearly everything from dinner to party ideas but you need to shift your mindset as it's **not just** recipes, DIY and home decor. You need to start thinking "how can I use this platform to better serve my customers and clients?".

Hopefully you have filled in the previous chapter's

exercise which will start to get you thinking about how you can serve your clients on Pinterest.

With this in mind, whilst you have been trying out Pinterest - did you find articles from business owners, did you find pins to purchase, did you find tips and tricks? Did you find a whole host of free value?

Don't get trying to fool me, I know the answer is YES. Now think back to your business and think could one of those pins have been yours?

- What is my ideal client typing in that search bar?
- How can you communicate to your ideal client through Pinterest?
- What can capture your audience's attention and then get them off the app to become a customer?

More on that shortly.

Firstly let's get it out there - its FREE! Yes free, zilch, nada, nothing! This platform that will do some amazing things for your business is totally free. So if I haven't said it already you really need to be investing time into getting a strategy together and using Pinterest as I know you will reap the rewards.

Pinterest is a growing platform. As I said it's at over 250 million users and that's a 40% increase on last year. The age range is broad with the majority between 25–54 and mostly women but more and more men are signing up. So regardless of your business or type of business I believe you can find your ideal clients/customers on Pinterest as it is serving everyone.

Pinterest is an opportunity for you to showcase your business to the right clients and customers using beautiful imagery. That's right, for you to target and put your content right in front of your ideal audience. Pinterest is designed to inspire and help people plan and buy. Don't you want to be on there showcasing what you have to offer?

Let's use an example here and say you make and sell candles. Pinterest gives you a platform to showcase beautiful pictures of your candles with the links to your shops and website.

Your potential clients can then click through to the shop or website or save your pin to use at a later date.

You might also blog about being a business owner, how you make your candles and local markets you attend.

You could also blog about the ingredients you use, how you source them and so on. You can create a great graphic to put on Pinterest that clicks back through to your blog post to help gain followers and engage your audience who want to see your content and love your business.

Sharing your own content can increase who views it, how many people engage with it and how many people follow you. Pinterest also makes it super simple to be able to attract the right audience and your ideal client to your website or to a call action by using specific pin descriptions, branding and the ideas and images that you pin.

In order to attract your ideal client you need to use a strategy and create pins purposely to direct traffic to your website.

More on this in the upcoming chapters.

Chapter Key Thoughts

- It's a free growing platform

- Attract the right audience to your site so you can convert them into an engaged audience
- Opportunity to showcase you and your business
- People come to Pinterest to be inspired, plan and buy

TARGET AUDIENCE

"SURROUND YOURSELF WITH PEOPLE WHO FORCE YOU TO LEVEL UP"

To attract the right audience to your site you need to know exactly who you are speaking to, attracting and pinning for so you can convert them into an engaged audience.

So first things first is identifying your client.

You might have already established your ideal client, in which case you're flying! If not, follow these steps to become super clear on who you are attracting.

1. Who are you speaking to?
2. What are they looking for?
3. How can you help them?
4. What brands do they follow?
5. Where do they shop?

6. Where are you going to send them?

7. How are you going to convert them to call to action?

When completing this exercise it helps to imagine an actual person that you have worked with in the past and that truly makes you passionate about what you do. Write down your answers to the above questions and be as specific and detailed as you can. It's important that you know his or her name, where they shop etc.

Based on this exercise you should be able to identify who you are pinning for. Let's pin what they want and need to see. Before you pin something for your target audience you need to think:

- Is this pin serving my ideal client?
- Will they value it or find it of use or interest?
- Is it adding value to what I offer?

If the answer is no then use secret boards to pin images for yourself. Remember your ideal clients aren't ready to buy but they are looking for a solution to their problem.

Other things you need to do to attract your ideal client is create a strong profile page, with the ability to quickly communicate your brand. Ensure your biography has keywords and clearly outlines who you serve and how you can help them. Make sure you verify your website, apply for rich pins and have a bio picture that's of you if it's your brand.

Here is an example of a great profile:

Kimberley Banner Social Media Mentor   1x Following
1.4m monthly unique viewers

🌐 www.kimberleybanner.com   I help Female Entrepreneurs create beautifully authentic & stand out profiles & to message with meaning. ✍️

Chapter Key Thoughts

- Identify your ideal client
- Make sure your content is serving your client
- Are your pins adding value to them?
- Create a strong profile page that quickly communicates how you can help them

HOW TO CREATE A KILLER CONTENT STRATEGY

"WITHOUT STRATEGY, CONTENT IS JUST STUFF"

So as with all other platforms, you need to ensure you have a strategy for your business and how you work. Pinterest is no different, it will work beautifully for you if you have a content strategy.

Here are some questions to help you think about your content:

- What are you going to create that will get re-pinned / go viral?
- Where is it going to link to?
- How are you going to convert the pins to website traffic or sales?
- How can you create beautiful graphics?
- Who is going to be searching?

- What keywords might be used?
- Invite people to take action

Note here the types of content you can create.

WHAT ARE YOU GOING TO CREATE THAT WILL GET RE-PINNED / GO VIRAL?

What content do you already make that you can re-purpose? Do you post on social media? Are you blogging? Do you have an Etsy shop or sell a product? Do you write articles? Do you have a podcast? All of this content can be re-purposed into a beautiful graphic to share on Pinterest.

The example below is of a blog post:

WHERE IS IT GOING TO LINK TO?

Your pins can link to anywhere. You can link them to a Facebook community, Instagram account, website, blog post and so on.

The above pin example linked directly to their website so they could increase their website traffic and get more interest in their program. Once users move from the Pinterest platform to your website you are more likely to get them on your email list.

HOW ARE YOU GOING TO CONVERT THE PINS?

Pinterest is beautiful and you can get lost in the pretty pictures. But your strategy needs to ensure that you are converting your pins. This could be moving them off the app to your website, joining an email list, joining a Facebook community or to an Etsy store or buying something from you.

It's from here that you will build engaged audiences and raving fans who are more likely to purchase from you and keep coming back. This could be easily done through the text in the graphic or description or by the link it takes them to. Ensure that you use specific descriptions with keywords and that the link it takes them to is not broken and is relevant to the pin.

Focussing on pinning for your ideal audience will gain views and engagement but you also need to ensure that you are planning for converting those pins. Think about the language you use as it needs to be written from the user's perspective so they can see how your product / service will help them. I would also recommend having your prices on your website. Remember it's all about the client - you want it to be easy for the client to work with you or buy your product.

Lastly clients that come to your site won't necessarily buy first time. You want to ensure they come back to you and remember you in the future. To do this you need to grab their attention! Create a brilliant freebie that prompts them to join your mailing list. Stay engaged with this audience as the opportunity for them to return to you to buy is down to you being in the front of their mind when they need it.

HOW CAN YOU CREATE BEAUTIFUL GRAPHICS?

No, you don't need a photo shoot! You can take great images from your smart phone these days but you do need good quality and well-lit pictures. Try and batch your work by planning a complete day where you focus on photography. Think about the backgrounds for you or your product, the lighting (you can make or get some great value light boxes) and you want that golden hour light before 10am or after 3pm. Regarding editing there are super easy apps you can use so have a play and choose which one you get along with best.

With regard to editing the graphic and making it pinnable, I would recommend using something like Canva. Canva is really easy to use, gives great filter options and editing options. It also gives you ready made Pinterest templates so you don't have to worry about sizing.

Your pins need to be portrait orientation, at least 735 pixels wide (but can be longer) and use good quality images. Using a portrait picture will convert more pins than a landscape picture as in the Pinterest feed a landscape picture isn't seen as easily.

Make sure you use easy to read typography and warm colours as they are more attractive to click on than cool colours. And make sure it's on brand! Use your colours and images to build a brand and visual identity that represents you and your business - this will attract your target audience. Canva can help you to keep it simple by adding your brand colours, typography and style into its inventory so you can easily use it at any time.

Ensure the Pins you are making are attractive and that in a feed full of pins it is yours that will make your ideal client stop and click on the image. We want your clients to stop and take action on your pin by ultimately clicking on it.

THE WOMAN I'M *Becoming*

I had the honour of capturing the Authors & Co book launch for 'The Woman I'm Becoming' - a friendly, re-assuring and positive guide for teenage girls as they approach life's challenges and crossroads.

SARAHSTONE.ONLINE

WHAT IS GOING TO BE SEARCHED?

For some of you this will be easy to figure out, but think back to when you started out in your business. What did you research? What did you need in order to progress? What were you reading? What help and solutions were you looking for?

These are all questions that need to be considered for your Pinterest. If you are not sure, use the search bar in Pinterest and this will give you examples of what else people are searching for. Make a list of everything that you think will be searched. This gives you examples of content that you can create for your client.

So for example, someone looking for a health coach might search health coach business, health coach career, health coach holistic, health coach quotes and so on.

WHAT WORDS MIGHT BE USED?

Having thought about your brand and business, what do you represent? Are you a female entrepreneur, in coaching or marketing? Do you sell products? Are you a small business owner?

These are all words that can be used as a search term and also in your pin descriptions. Using the correct words will also ensure your Pin comes up in the user's searches and also help your Search Engine Optimisation.

So let's go back to our candle business as an example. When searching for candles Pinterest recommends keywords such as DIY, Yankee, homemade, crafts, luxury, ideas etc. These are all words that you need to use in your descriptions and boards to ensure your content comes through in a search.

INVITE PEOPLE TO TAKE ACTION

What action do you want people to take when they click on your pin? You need to ensure that each pin is asking or telling your audience to do something.

Actions could include:

- Joining a Facebook community
- Following an Instagram account
- Continuing to website for article or blog
- Joining an email list
- Making contact

It is important to get your audience off the app and to ask them to take action. If you fail to implement this step you will be missing out on growing your audience and building raving fans.

If you are consistent with this step you will build your brand to be trusted and known thus making it easier to convert your clients.

Chapter Key Thoughts

- Have beautiful, quality graphics
- Ensure you use keywords
- Ensure you are asking your audience to take action

PINNING MARKETING STRATEGY

"QUALITY IS THE BEST BUSINESS PLAN"

In order to ensure you see results on Pinterest you need to implement a pinning marketing strategy. You have nailed your content strategy so now when do you pin? With everything it's all about consistency so Pinterest will reward you for pinning consistently.

You can use platforms such as Tailwind to help you with this. It can recommend the best times of day to pin and create a schedule for you to look at your results/analytics and decide when to pin. Personally I would recommend investing in Tailwind as you can plan weeks in advance. Head over to my website for a quick demonstration on how to use Tailwind.

The first 5 pins of each day need to be your content as these are the first from you that your audience will see.

Don't worry if you haven't got 5 pieces of content a day yet, but try to build a suite of your own content to share.

This can include pinning to several boards and having the same content but with different images e.g. blog post but several different graphics for the same blog post. And where possible you need to add 'evergreen' content which will outlast dates and times and still be gaining you results long in to the future. Pinterest is also about sharing so make an effort to share other people's content too!

Don't get too hung up on this area to start with but just make sure you are consistent. It's not about quantity so if you can pin just 2 pins every day that is better than 14 on one day and none the next day.

Pinterest should be considered as a long-term strategy because of the longevity of the pins. A pin you share today can be seen years later and still be bringing in several hundred views or continually adding subscribers to your email list. So make sure you think about this as you plan out your content and graphics.

Here is a little guide to help you with what to do daily, weekly and monthly:

What to do daily

You need to pin 5 of your own or other's content per day. Check the home feed to like and re-pin any relevant content.

What to do weekly

Check out any of your new followers and follow back but only if relevant. Find some new pinners to follow that share good quality content. Take a day to batch your work and create new images for Pinterest. Glance at analytics only to see how your Pinterest is doing but don't get too hung up on the numbers.

What to do monthly

Once a month I recommend you schedule out your evergreen content. If you use Tailwind this is super simple. Review your Pinterest analytics and take a deep dive into what has been working and what hasn't in order to make any changes. See what is trending and where you can add anything relevant for your audience.

Don't forget Pinterest is used for planning so Pinners will be searching in advance for inspiration. Lastly, review your Google analytics and see if you are redirecting your audience from the app to your website. Look at what articles or pages are getting the most views and then tweak accordingly.

Here is a content Pinning calendar of what to pin and when based on the trends Pinterest has shown.

January
Spring Cleaning
Healthy Recipes
Valentine's Day
Organisation Tips
Spring Break
Fitness

February
Spring Break
St. Patrick's Day
Comfort Food
Spring Fashions
Spring Cleaning
Tax Help

March
Easter
Pastels

Gardening
Outdoor Fun
Travel
Budgeting
Floral Patterns

April

Graduation
Weddings
Travel
Mother's Day
Fitness
Summer Fashion
Healthy Foods

May

Swim Suits
Summer Recipes
Summer Weddings
Outdoors/Camping
Healthy Foods
Father's Day

June

4th of July

Weekend Getaways
Baby Showers
Gardening
BBQ
Holidays
Swim Fashion

July

Summer BBQ Recipes
Back-to-School Organisation
Summer Cocktails
Vacation & Travel
Summer Weddings
Gardening
Christmas in July
Boredom Busters

August

Back-to-School
Fall Fashion
Camping
Organisation & Routine Tips
Grilling Recipes
Autumn/Fall Weddings
Halloween

September

Comfort Food

Football Food

Preserving

Halloween

Autumn/Fall Weddings

Holiday Budgeting

Thanksgiving

Family Photos

October

Autumn/Fall Foods

Halloween

Family Photos

Crocktober

Thanksgiving

Travel Tips

Christmas

Winter Fashion

November

Thanksgiving

Christmas

Hanukkah

Dinner Parties

Travel
Black Friday
Cyber Monday
Gift Guides

December
Christmas
Party Planning
New Year's Resolutions
Winter Décor
Hanukkah
Winter Weddings
Holiday Fashion
Travel

The list above should help start the creative juices flowing of how your business can show up on Pinterest and be amongst the trends.

PinTip -

Look at the most popular Pins on your account this month, if any of them are NOT your content could you create a similar if not better piece of content and pin that? Also focus on your descriptions a little more, they need to be short and sweet, keyword rich and include hashtags. Complete a search to see what's popular with your audience.

Chapter Key Thoughts

- Pin consistently; daily if possible
- You can use platforms such as Tailwind to help with scheduling
- Try and pin your content as the first 5 pins
- Use the content calendar to give you ideas of what to pin and when

"YOUR BRAND IDENTITY TELLS PEOPLE
WHO YOU ARE, WHAT YOU DO, WHY YOU
DO IT AND HOW YOU DO IT"

Branding is personal and therefore your Pinterest should be easily recognisable as **YOU**. Your personal brand is unique to you therefore it should show your values as a business or entrepreneur.

Confused people won't buy from you so you need to make sure that you are absolutely clear on what you offer and how you can help them.

Your own pins, your boards and your bio must all tie into your brand. Just like an Instagram board or website, your Pinterest account needs to be an extension of this.

In Canva you can add your colour hex codes and import images so you can easily and cheaply keep your style and Pinterest on brand. If using Canva, make sure you use this function to easily keep your typography and colours consistent.

That way you and your brand will be easily recognisable in a feed full of pins and be relevant to your audience. Ensure that you have a logo or picture of yourself and a well written bio telling your audience how you can help them.

Have a look at some of the accounts at the back of this book for great examples of how to make your Pinterest specific to your brand.

Chapter Key Thoughts

- Be consistent with brand
- Ensure your Pinterest account has the same look and feel as your Instagram and website
- Share other people's content that is in keeping with your brand

THE IMPORTANCE OF SEARCH ENGINE OPTIMISATION (SEO)

"GOOGLE ONLY LOVES YOU WHEN EVERYONE ELSE LOVES YOU FIRST"

I t's POWERFUL for you to remember that Pinterest is a SEARCH ENGINE like Google and not a social media platform like Facebook.

WHAT IS SEO?

You may have no idea what SEO (Search Engine Optimisation) means. Well, put simply it's about organising your content effectively so that when people search a relevant word, you show up in their search results and therefore improving your search engine rankings.

Let's not forget that Pinterest is a search engine like Google so it's really important to optimise all your content both on Pinterest and your website to make sure you are improving your rankings.

On a website you add plug-ins to help ensure that you are optimising your content. On Pinterest the main way you can optimise your content is to consistently use relevant keywords.

People use Google and Pinterest in the same way - by searching for a term or word. You will want to ensure that you come up in the search results when they are searching for a specific word.

Keywords within Pinterest are the words you use to describe the pin, feature, item and your business. In the same way that hashtags work on Instagram, these keywords will start to build up a picture on Pinterest so that when someone searches for a word your content appears in the search results.

3 ways to help optimise your content –

1. Create beautiful, valuable and informative content
2. Use words or phrases that are easily searched by your audience
3. Make it easy to share it!

KEYWORDS

Just like you would search in Google, start to type any of your keyword ideas in to Pinterest and it will give you further ideas on what people are searching for.

For example when I typed in the search bar 'become an author' it also showed me – 'Book, Writers, Writing, Articles, Products'. These could all be examples of other keywords I could use if I was sharing my content on Becoming an Author.

Another search I completed was 'Candles'. It also suggested 'Making, how to make, DIY, homemade, Decorative'.

So now take some time and brainstorm keywords that are relevant to your business. Don't forget to use Pinterest to give you ideas of what is already being searched for.

If you're really stuck use the keyword explorer here to help. https://moz.com/explorer

Chapter Key Thoughts

- Pinterest is a visual search engine
- SEO is optimising your content to show up in a search result
- Use keywords – they're so important!

NETWORK

"COLLABORATE WITH PEOPLE YOU CAN LEARN FROM"

As with other platforms Pinterest does have a 'follower' count. These are the people that follow your account to receive notifications of when you have pinned new content, to see your content automatically in their feed and on the 'following' tab.

As I have said before your content will be searchable to anyone even if they don't follow you. So my advice to you is don't get hung up on your number of followers.

You might find your following number is low but actually your monthly figures are high. Work on providing quality content that your ideal audience want and need and in time your count will rise.

Pinterest is a bit of a slow burner. Usually it will take a couple of months before you see an impact in your stats. I would suggest you use a tracker to keep a record of any changes you make and pins you add so you know why you might have changes in your views or following.

You should keep track of your monthly unique views and who engages with your content. These are the important figures with regard to getting your content in front of your audience.

Don't be afraid to network with other people on Pinterest. You might find local businesses that you support or fellow entrepreneurs in your industry.

As I have said before it's collaboration over competition so if you can network and share content with others then why not?

Also when pinning don't forget to grab fans for your other platforms such as Instagram or Facebook. You could be pinning with a link specifically to one of those platforms.

And lastly you can sell on Pinterest! If you have a product, a shop or a service create a beautiful pin directing your audience to the sales page which clearly explains in the description (using keywords) how you can serve them.

Chapter Key Thoughts

- Use Pinterest to network
- Don't worry about your follower count!
- Don't forget you can sell

ANALYTICS

"WE MUST MOVE FROM NUMBERS
KEEPING SCORE TO NUMBERS THAT
DRIVE BETTER ACTIONS" - DAVID
WALMSLEY

With a business account you will get the added extra of being able to use and analyse your results. You will see in your profile there is a tab called Analytics - these Analytics are your data and results from your Pinterest account showing you what is working and what needs improving.

There are several areas to Analytics.

'Overview' gives you a quick look at your profile, people you reach and your website.

Within your Pinterest profile analytics you will see the average daily impressions and average daily viewers for a time period. You will also see what your top pin impressions and top board impressions are. This gives you good insight into what boards are popular and what pins are working well.

There are also tabs called 'save' and 'clicks'. These are the saves from your Pinterest profile and the click throughs to your website.

The 'people you reach' tab will give you your average monthly viewers and average monthly engaged. This means x amount of people saw your content (viewers) and x amount of people actually did something with it (engaged).

A really great tool to utilise is your 'audience insights'. This report tells you who is seeing your Pinterest content, who is engaging, how old they are, their gender, their location etc. You can see from this report whether your strategy is finding your ideal client. You can also download this into an Excel document to keep track of the data.

Analytics can seem a bit overwhelming but don't let yourself get worried over it. Log in and have a look at your stats but don't worry too much over the figures, the general trends will guide you to improve your content. Personally I would take note of what pins and boards are doing well and your audience insights. Your monthly viewers and engaged audience will fluctuate depending on if a pin has gone viral or if you have made any changes so don't worry if this goes up and down.

Chapter Key Thoughts

- Stats can seem overwhelming but log in and take a look
- Take note of what pins and boards are doing well
- Gives insight into your audience
- Use this to change your content strategy if needed

AUTOMATION

"YOU'RE EITHER THE ONE THAT CREATES AUTOMATION, OR YOU ARE GETTING AUTOMATED" – TOM PRESTON-WARNER

Pinterest doesn't need to be another laborious task to add to your list. You can manage your Pinning Strategy with just 15 minutes or so a week.

As mentioned earlier, I use and recommend the platform Tailwind. Tailwind is an automation system that lets you manage and get results from Pinterest and Instagram.

Tailwind picks the best times to post for your audience so there is no need to be pinning live and it is really easy to use with simple video tutorials explaining how to use it. You can try it for free with up to 100 pins. It allows you to schedule your pins at a date and time for weeks in advance.

There are two main schedules available – 'smart schedule' which optimises the times or 'custom schedule'. You can add as many or as little time slots as you want.

You can upload your own content or re-pin other people's content. With Tailwind you can stay consistent without being on Pinterest all of the time. Tailwind lets you directly pin from Instagram so if there are items on Instagram you want to share you have that option. You can also link your Facebook pages and share to those to.

There is also an option called 'smart loop' which lets you set up your best content to be shared to Pinterest indefinitely, saving you time and increasing your traffic to your website.

Tailwind has what it calls 'tribes' which are groups of pins in different niches and industries. You can share your pin to any tribe but you must follow the rules. With tribes you can increase your re-pins and grow your following.

On Tailwind there is an analytics tab which gives you information on your performance of your boards, most re-pinned pin, your followers and the engagement with the pins. It's worth looking at this area as it will give insight into how to improve your Pinterest and traffic to your website.

Chapter Key Thoughts:

- Tailwind is a useful automation system
- It allows you to schedule as many pins as you like
- Use the analytics to view your performance and where you can improve

CONVERSION

"IMPROVE YOUR CONVERSIONS AND DOUBLE YOUR BUSINESS"

With Pinterest the aim is to get click throughs to your website which will get you traffic, email subscribers, raving fans and clients; otherwise known as conversions.

To help improve your conversions add your graphic into your website and then pin it from your website. For example, you have written a blog, so create a beautiful graphic, add the graphic into your blog in your website, then 'pin it' from your website to your Pinterest account.

Don't forget to fill in the 'alt text' box with a keyword description as this will enhance your SEO and when anyone else saves your pin this is the description that is used.

The way you use SEO in your website and set it up in your content and layout will have a direct effect on Pinterest. If your content isn't appealing or doesn't have a good description or headline then it won't show up in searches and people won't click through.

I'm really hoping that once you put in all that hard work outlined above, Pinterest will become your number 1 traffic referral route to your website and blog.

Now to be clear Pinterest is all about visuals and the beautiful imagery BUT ultimately, we want to get our ideal client off the platform and to our website or to somewhere else where we can manage them better. Your website is like the sales funnel or your showroom and Pinterest is how they enter.

There are several ways to do this and measure this.

Firstly I would recommend you add Google analytics or another analytics source to your website. Quite quickly you will be able to see where your traffic is coming from, what pages they are spending time looking at and where within your website. It will also show where you lose traffic which will help you with your content strategy and perhaps where you should be spending more or even less time!

LEAD MAGNET/LANDING PAGES/OPT INS

A landing page or lead magnet is a webpage that appears in response to clicking on a graphic or image and can be used to sell a product or service. You can post the link to this page within Pinterest so that it directs users straight there.

You need to build 'like, know and trust' with your audience. Your dream client who is following you and all of your content wants to know you, they want to like you and they need to trust you. They will also like a quick win so that's where your lead magnet is so helpful as you can give your dream client a bonus such as a freebie, cheat sheet etc.

You need to ensure you have a core lead magnet. A core lead magnet is what you put front and centre on your website to get your dream client to sign up to your email list. The core lead magnet needs to address your dream client's problem. It needs to represent your brand and have a fairly large reach.

Ask yourself what does my dream client always ask me

online, or what are they looking for? You need to be giving away massive value and even question yourself why you are giving it away for free!

With lead magnets you need to have a strategy so what is your end game, what are you going to sell? You need to make sure you have this nailed so the lead magnet can align with the product, program or service you are going to sell. So what does your dream client need to understand to ensure they are equipped to purchase?

Think about these questions when you are creating your core lead magnet:

Does it provide an answer to your dream client's problem?

Does it deliver a quick win for your dream client?

Does it give an idea of what you want to sell and leaves the dream client wanting more?

Does it build 'like, know and trust' with your client?

Remember to keep your core lead magnet simple. Save any video series or podcasts to your promotional lead magnets. For your promotional lead magnets, i.e. where you are promoting a specific product or service, you can use items such as video masterclass, audio training, webinars.

Remember with an opt-in (a giveaway/freebie someway of them joining your list) you need to show your audience you can solve a problem they have and be specific on what that is.

HOW TO INCREASE YOUR LIST BUILDING?

List building is a way of increasing the number of people who get your email. Ways to increase your list building effort can include doing a Facebook live, Facebook group, Instagram promotion and of course Pinterest! Other ways are by putting an opt in form on your header in your website, on the sidebar and within your posts.

The more you repeat the more likely you will get the purchase or sale but don't forget you need to offer different ways of saying things without sounding 'spammy'. The key to all conversions is that in order to sell, you have to offer value. Serve your audience by giving them free content - serve, serve, serve and then sell -you are more likely to convert your audience into paying clients this way.

LEAD MAGNET CONTENT IDEAS

These ideas should help you when creating your lead page. Focus on the content i.e. what value you are giving rather than in what form it is.

Firstly you could provide the following:

How to

Recommendations

Questions – that you know your audience are asking

Step by step – blueprint

Teasers – if you have something already made you can pull from this

Tips – expert tips – reach out to people

Behind the scenes – toolkit, give away exact questions or exact document on a process

Newsletter – don't use just because you need to make sure it is giving away value that your audience wants to read time and time again such as Join the revolution, get a downloadable document, top tips for... and so on.

Ok so these are all types of information you could

provide to your clients; now what form do you give it in?

Ideas can include:

Cheat sheet

Checklist

Guide

Blueprint – map idea

File – copy language

Audio – know, like and trust

So now marry the two – what is the best packaging for your content? Remember to keep it simple, that way you will get it done and provide a quick win for your clients.

Cheat sheet or checklist – this is an easy quick tool to provide to your clients.

Show and tell – this could include a how to and show them results.

Guide or file -this could be a blue print or top tips.

Audio – This could be any of the how to's or recommendations.

You need to ensure that in exchange for a person signing up to your email list you are giving value. An opt-in can be anything such as a free e-book, a report, a free resource, 5 top tips to getting a killer Pinterest profile and so on. What content could you create that ensures your dream client signs up to get your freebie?

The point of your lead magnet is to get the person from Pinterest to your resource and then on to your email list. Pinterest is an amazing tool at driving traffic to your website but you have to put things in place to ensure you capture the traffic and ultimately get them to stay.

The free resources you provide don't have to be huge but they do have to provide value. You need to ask yourself is this of value to my client and will they sign up to my email list in order to get more of this type of content. They need to be saying 'Wow I can't believe this is free!'

An opt-in is a quick win and a way to build your email list organically via Pinterest. You need to make sure that your conversion strategy ties in with your overall strategy i.e. you write a blog, you create a beautiful graphic in the blog and pin to Pinterest.

The graphic leads them back to your website where you are giving a free resource, in order to get the free resource they join your email list. Once you have the hang of this the rewards will be endless and you will see growth in your list building.

Chapter Key Thoughts:

- The aim is to use Pinterest to get traffic to your website
- Use a core lead magnet to get people signed up
- Use a cheat sheet or a checklist as a quick win

EMAIL LIST

"YOU OWN YOUR EMAIL LIST, NO ONE ELSE"

Ok so now on to the list! If you don't have an email list then other than joining Pinterest this needs to be top of your things to do! An email list is a way of managing clients, your tribe and people who just want your free content.

You might have thousands of followers on Instagram and Pinterest but you **DON'T OWN** these - Mark Zuckerberg and the like do! Did you know that only 6% of your social media posts are actually seen by your audience? I know you can do better than that with a list.

Research shows that over 50% of people check their inbox first thing in the morning -we as human beings don't like to miss anything! This means that the average open rate on emails is between 20% and 40%!

On the other hand, you do own your email list. You own how often you email, what content you share, how many people are in different groups and so on. Personally the only number I worry about is how many people are receiving my emails! The message in an email is five times more likely to be read than seen on Facebook. With email you can build a stronger relationship with your ideal client and be more personal to them.

With an email list you can provide value, resources, content and **SELL**! This is where you will turn your fans into clients and your traffic into sales.

Pinterest will drive your traffic and you will probably be amazed at how much traffic it can create. After all we humans are nosy! But you need to keep them once they've found you as it's unlikely that you will consistently sell from Pinterest without moving users on to an email list or through an opt-in first.

Did you know that 66% of marketers said that their email list delivers an excellent return on investment, 66% of consumers have made a purchase online as a result of an email marketing message and email marketing contributes to 30% of all digital revenues! So why are you not using it?

You need to have a list building strategy. Without a strategy your emails could get to the inbox but never be opened! Ensure you plan your content and take advantage of going direct to the inbox. Remember that those on your email list won't be ready to buy but they are looking for a solution to their immediate problem otherwise they wouldn't have joined your list looking for answers. The average click through rate is 2.43% - this is how many people get an email and click. Compare that to Facebook adverts and the click through rate is 0.90%! So hopefully you can see the value in building an email list!

There are plenty of free email list providers such as Mail Chimp, Convert Kit and Active Host. Review which one will work best for you and your business and then set up your email templates. You need to have a thank you sequence, welcome sequence and your lead magnet sequence.

HOW TO GENERATE TRAFFIC WITH EMAILS

Your emails need to be emails that will be opened not just deleted! Have you already got a list but they're not opening to read? Have a think about emails that you open - what is the subject line, how does it get your attention?

Think about what is the number one question you get asked by your clients, what are they embarrassed to admit, what solution do you have for them, what do they need to know about you, what should they be asking you and aren't, what expert's opinion matters to them, what have they tried in the past that didn't work.

Use this space to brain storm your ideas. Remember you need to make sure you have an end result for your client, what is this email meant to do - provide value or sell.

You need to have a strong subject line. Hopefully you have some ideas above but here is a list of email subject lines that might help you.

Create curiosity

5 things they didn't know about you

The secret to ....

The most common mistakes every ....

Make it personal

I made a video for you

This is for you

First name, what do you think of this

Urgency

25% off today only!

Cart closes in 24 hours!

15 spots left

Free shipping Sunday only!

Teach

My cheat sheet for ....

5 tips to solve .....

How to ...

Use numbers

7 simple things to do to increase ...

3 tips to increase revenue by ...

101 things to do before you ....

Tell a story

If I started all over again, I would

This one thing changed ....

Before I crashed and burned I did ...

Lead with headlines

7 ways to attract new clients (Webinar)

Tonight only – live with ...

The results from....

BATCH CONTENT

I'm sure you have heard of this before but you will be far more productive if you batch your content. You need to plan out your emails for the next quarter and year and then write the content. You can make an image to go with it for Pinterest and your social media and then all you have to do is schedule!

It is far easier to batch your content as you will be more productive than if you go from one thing to another. Use the above exercise to start decide on your subject lines and then plan out when it is relevant to post.

CALL TO ACTION

Each email along with each Pin needs to have a call to action. What do you want your dream client or audience to do? This should be in bold and easily seen so they are more likely to do what you asked. Is this email to fill up a webinar, sell a product, adding value? Make sure it links back to your end goal.

The call to action doesn't need to be a big thing or sound spammy. You could reference one of your podcasts, your Instagram or Facebook community or a resource.

Chapter Key Thoughts:

- You need to have an email list and a list building strategy
- Use strong headlines to get your emails opened
- Batch content – have an email writing day!
- Always use a call to action

WAYS TO BUILD YOUR LIST

"GO THE EXTRA MILE IT'S NEVER CROWDED"

SOCIAL MEDIA AND PUBLIC RELATIONS

Social media is a sure way to boost your email list efforts along with Pinterest. What's popular at the moment is Facebook live, Facebook groups, Instagram and stories, Pinning on Pinterest, and advertising on any of those platforms.

Also have you ever thought about paying to advertise your freebies? This is a great way to build your email list and you can reap serious numbers for your email list.

Also utilising Public Relations (PR) will do great things for your business including building your list!

You need to work on how to pitch yourself to successfully secure those PR opportunities.

Work with a PR agency if you can or if not, you need to work on your elevator pitch and be able to successfully pitch yourself to magazines, newspapers and other bloggers to share your story.

POP UP METHOD

Use a pop up or install a 'join my email list' box on your website and make sure you don't give any free resources without them joining your list first. With a pop-up box use a timer so it doesn't pop up straight away and annoy your potential client! And make sure it is with your core lead magnet.

You can also use the pop-up box in other ways such as on content upgrades, thank you pages and so on. Just be sure to place them appropriately so they don't pop up when your potential client is trying to read content.

PINTEREST

Use Pinterest to generate the traffic to your site so you can convert your clients effortlessly! You can share your graphics and content on Pinterest to build up your email list. This could be a pin for a specific blog or podcast where the link takes them to your website and they can then join your list via a pop-up box or content upgrade.

Or you make a pin for my '5 Top tips for using your business' and then the link takes them to your core lead magnet. You can also use promoted pins to advertise your freebies and get numbers on your email list.

FREEBIES

The ideas you made for your lead content pages will be great ways to add to your list. You need to ensure that whenever offering something for free you get their email address. Get a bit more creative and think "what does my ideal client really want?". Maybe up the game a bit to ensure you are offering something so valuable they have to sign up to your list!

LAUNCH

Launches will usually bring an influx of subscribers to your email list. Whether you are offering a freebie, product or service why not think about different ways to offer this up. For example you could do a webinar and to join they sign up with your list. Make sure you offer seriously valuable information and that way you will retain your subscriber.

Chapter Key Thoughts

- Pinterest can be your main source for traffic to your website
- Give thought to your lead pages and what value you can give away for free
- Don't over complicate your lead pages or freebies – keep it simple!
- Ways to build your list include social media, PR, freebies and launches.

BLOGGING

"WRITE SOMETHING WORTH READING"

A blog is a tool that can increase your online presence, attract traffic and engage with your ideal audience. You may think that you have missed the boat on blogging, but that's just not true. Blogging and content marketing still represent the third biggest marketing tool with Pinterest first and social media as second.

Blogging is a little different now, you can't rely on your blog to make your income but it needs to be part of your overall strategy to get people to your website.

With blogging you need to ensure to provide value. The topic you are writing about needs to solve a problem for your audience or provide some information they need. My tips for anyone starting out with a blog would be to write like you talk, be consistent and blog often, make your point again and again, take some time to edit your post and then you need to hit publish!! Make it personal - blogging should be fun for you and engaging for your audience to read.

With your blogs ensure you make them optimised and they will show up in Google and Pinterest. You can add long or short keywords but the best places to make sure they show up are within your title, on the URL, on any images you produce and within the post. With a blog post you want to make sure you have an opt-in for your email too.

On Pinterest you can share a good image with a clear title and a well written description with your keywords and that will help the click through rate to your website.

Ensure each of your posts have structure to them, with a header, an image and not too long sentences. If you write with a structure and plan and stay consistent it will be more likely that a reader stays on that page. For your design layout make sure the background is lighter as it makes for easier reading.

Setting up a blog is easy. Choose a great name and find a web host for your site. WordPress offer free hosting and have tons of help, plug ins and are the most popular for blogging. WordPress also offer help on your design and easier ways to manage your search engine optimisation.

With all your blog posts make sure you are using keywords appropriately and effectively.

Chapter Key Thoughts:

- Blogging is a way of sharing your story and entrepreneur journey
- Pinterest is a great way for sharing your blogs
- Structure your posts with headers, images and short sentences
- Use keywords to become effective in the searches

PROMOTED PINS

"GOOD THINGS COME TO THOSE WHO HUSTLE"

Promoted pins are pins that businesses pay to promote or advertise. The promoted pins you see as a user are based on your activity on Pinterest or on that advertiser's site. As with other platforms if you don't want to see a promoted pin you can hide it.

To enable promoted pins you have to pay for them to be placed where your audience will most likely see them. These pins can then be placed in your audience's feed and search results.

You will need a business account to create promoted pins and the amount you pay will depend on the budget you set. You can promote pins to a certain audience or factor. To create promoted pins go to the Advert manager at the top of your Pinterest.

You will first start with creating a campaign. To create a new campaign, name it first and set your budget. Then move onto the advert setup and edit that. Pinterest will allow you to promote the pin based on demographics such as gender, location and gender.

As we have already talked about keywords are really important here. Pinterest will target your promoted pin based on their keyword advertising method to ensure it is targeted and effective. You can add up to 150 keywords so this makes sure you are more competitive. Try and think outside of the box and add relevant keywords that your audience might be searching for.

Make sure you choose a pin to promote that is attractive and a good quality image. With Pinterest it is all about the images so make sure you can catch your audience's attention first.

This pin needs to get your audience to take action. It needs to convey your idea, product or service. With promoted pins you need to ensure you use rich pins. There are up to 6 different types of rich pins and you will need some help from your web developer to insert the code.

The image will attract your audience first but make sure you are making the most out of your description. It needs to explain what the image is and why they should click through. I wouldn't use hashtags here. You don't want your audience clicking on the hashtag and being taken away from your pin.

Timing is really important with any advertising. You may like to use holidays such as Christmas, Easter or Black Friday. But you can use any time you wish such as Mother's Day. Once your campaign is live, you need to track your results and make notes for the next time you promote a pin.

Don't be afraid to do split testing to work out what is better for your audience. I recommend trying different graphics and messages to see what works better. You can create multiple adverts under the same campaign so this will allow you to test different factors and track the results.

Make sure your landing page or link you're referring them to is what they are expecting. You don't want any random links such as your home page or random lead page, you want them to be sent to exactly what the promoted pin is about.

If you don't your audience will likely get frustrated and click away even if they were interested in your product or service before.

Lastly if you can use video. This will ensure your promoted pin stands out from the rest of the pins.

Chapter Key Thoughts:

- Promoted pins are ways of advertising
- Just like advertising you have to pay
- Keywords are really important to your campaign
- Use video if you can; if not a really good quality image

CREATE RAVING FANS

"CREATE A TRIBE OF RAVING FANS"

Pinterest is a place for you to create a tribe of raving fans. Just like on social media, you can increase followers so that your fans get notified when you post.

To create raving fans you need to provide content that your ideal clients want to see. That way your fans will become your followers. Having said that don't worry about what your follower number is you need to worry about what your click through rate is.

Get your fans off the app and over to your website, you need to provide your fans with the content they want to read, watch and buy.

When you do get your fans off the app and over to

your website you want to keep them there. Ensure your website loads quickly and has an easy to use menu so your fans can navigate around it easily. You also want to make sure that it's very clear what you do and how you can help them.

Chapter Key Thoughts:

- Get your fans off the app and build a tribe!

VALUE FOR YOUR COMMUNITY

"COMMUNITY OVER COMPETITION"

You need to provide value! Value over sales and value over competition. In your emails provide value such as engagement, encouragement and information. Make sure you provide value before selling anything.

If you use a blog make sure it is informative and helpful.

With Pinterest you need to make sure you are adding pins that are of value to your community. Think about what and why you are pinning to make sure it engages your community.

Don't forget to post other people's content but make sure it's valuable to your audience.

Chapter Key Thoughts:

- Add content that is valuable for your community and audience
- Provide loads of value before you sell anything

GROWTH FOR BUSINESS

"DREAMS DON'T WORK UNLESS YOU DO"

With Pinterest you can see a massive increase in your traffic to your website resulting in growth for your business.

If you take the steps required as outlined in this book, you will be rewarded.

Pinterest doesn't have to be time consuming but you are missing out if you don't use it at all for your business.

Pinterest drives over 33% more traffic than Facebook; if you are using social media than you need to use Pinterest too.

Make sure to get your audience off Pinterest and on to

your email list. Offer them something that they can't believe is free to get signed up.

Chapter Key Thoughts:

- If you use Pinterest correctly you will be rewarded
- It will increase your traffic thus growing your business

CREATING A CUSTOMER EXPERIENCE

"CUSTOMERS MAY FORGET WHAT YOU SAID, BUT THEY WON'T FORGET HOW YOU MADE THEM FEEL"

All of us in business need to pay attention to the customer experience. Pinterest is no different. If a customer has a good experience with you they will come back and recommend you.

Make sure with Pinterest that you are on brand and your links work. There is nothing more frustrating than to click on a pin and the link is broken.

You also want to ensure that the link you are taking them to is relevant to your pin.

When potential customers arrive at your website make sure it runs smoothly and that they can opt in to your email list.

Chapter Key Thoughts:

- Pay attention to your customer
- Recommendations are key
- Make everything recognisable as your brand

AFFILIATE MARKETING

"PASSIVE INCOME IS THE KEY TO FINANCIAL FREEDOM"

SO WHAT IS AFFILIATE MARKETING?

Basically it's recommending a product or service and getting paid a commission on sales. Every day we recommend a restaurant or book or product to our friends and family so why not get paid for doing so.

An example of affiliate marketing could be you're a make-up artist and blogger and use MAC cosmetics all the time. You could become a MAC Cosmetics affiliate so when you recommend your favourite products you get paid as a result of the sales. Commission ranges anywhere from 3% to 40%.

WHERE TO FIND THEM?

So to find affiliate programs you can either go direct to a merchant's site and at the bottom of the page see if there is 'affiliate' or 'become an affiliate' and then the company's program will be shown if they have one. Or you can join an affiliate programs network and get access to thousands of programs on their database.

AFFILIATE PROGRAM NETWORKS

There are lots of things you will want to consider when joining an affiliate program network such as their pay-out schedule, the type of affiliates they have and if they offer support such as an account manager.

Examples of affiliate program networks are:

- ShareAsale
- Ultimate Bundles
- CJ Affiliates

There are lots of networks available once you start exploring this area but be careful as some are more US driven than others. Most people avoid using Amazon affiliates on Pinterest because it is not clear if it is allowed or not so err on the side of caution with this merchant.

HOW TO USE IT ON PINTEREST

On Pinterest pretty much any links work well. Have a look at your boards and see what affiliate links you have shared without knowing it. What could you share that links well with what your business or blog is all about? Ask yourself "what would my audience like to buy"? Examples are:

- Mummy Blogs/Childcare – create boards such as children life hacks, snacks for kids, children's clothes then you can pin your favourite products with affiliate links.
- Craft/DIY – link your fave products, inspiration and tools that you use.
- Fashion bloggers – these can work really well. Pin your favourite t-shirts, sunglasses, bikinis, jeans and so on.

Don't be spammy! You want to make sure you are sharing products or services that are of value to your audience. Don't just share a load of products with affiliate links and expect to get commission if it's not relevant to your audience. Be patient as this can take time but if you are sharing relevant products or services people will click on the pin.

Make sure you disclose that you are an affiliate on the pin. You can do this by editing the pin description and adding #afflink or #affiliate on all your pins. I would recommend you do this on every product or service you are affiliate for.

Also make sure your pin descriptions are really strong, straight to the point and concise as this will take them straight to the affiliate's site rather than your site or blog. Don't edit the link or make it shorter - use the link that is given to you.

Go through your existing pins and see if there are any pins that you can add any affiliate links to. This will help establish trust with your audience when you start pinning more affiliate links.

Create boards that are specifically for your affiliates. For example, tools and resources work really well so when somebody clicks on that pin they know they will be taken to where to purchase it.

Keep it on brand! The affiliate pins still need to be in keeping with your brand, colours and images. As discussed before use Canva to edit and make sure that the aesthetic of your Pinterest is still pleasing for your audience.

Some products or services will come with their own pinnable graphic but you will stand out from the crowd if you edit or make your own. And don't be afraid to make more than one pinnable graphic as you would with your own content.

However having said all that you really need to consider whether affiliate marketing is for you. If you have a product or service you really need to be promoting your own pins before promoting anyone else's.

Chapter Key Thoughts:

- Affiliate marketing is promoting other people's products to earn commission
- Take consideration into what affiliate marketing you do
- Keep it on brand!

FINAL THOUGHTS

So there you have it – my guide to Using Pinterest for conversions. You can do this! Pinterest should not take you any more time than 1-2 hours per week.

Some key things to remember are to be consistent. Pinterest will reward you for consistency. Be on brand and make your pin images beautiful so your audience will want to click on them.

Make sure you are building an email list and concentrate on that number building as you own your list!

There are several ways to build your list including Pinterest, social media and PR. And I'll say it again -

be consistent, find a way to build your list and stick with it.

I hope you will find Pinterest to be a successful tool for generating traffic and building those conversions in your business.

CASE STUDIES

RECENT CLIENTS

"I was reaching up to 2.8million views on my profile!"

Kimberley Banner

Kimberley Banner is a Social Media Coach and Mentor. She is an Instagram expert and offers one to one coaching and training for businesses and entrepreneurs. Kim got in contact with me as she wanted to get more traffic to her website and increase her online presence.

Kim started getting results and fast. With Kim's profile I was able to link her Instagram account and post from there. She quickly started seeing that Pinterest was her number one traffic source and more than Instagram itself!

Here is what Kimberley said about working with me.

"Ally is an absolute ray of sunshine to work with & made Pinterest really easy to understand from a client point of view. I left Ally to her own devices & she reported back with monthly statistics to show me how my brand was performing so I knew what kind of content was working.

My Pinterest has grown significantly in a very short space of time. I was reaching monthly views on my profile of up to 2.8 million which is unbelievable!

Ally really helped get my brand out there & I converted followers pinning my work to paying clients. Ally is a really beautiful person & an asset to your business with her vast knowledge of both business & Pinterest. An amazing investment & one that really pays off.

I regularly get messages from people seeing my brand on Pinterest & also get people I don't know tagging me in my work material over on Instagram - they had found my content on Instagram. Thank you so much for your contribution to my business growth Ally - you're amazing!"

Female Success Network

Female Success Network specialise in helping female entrepreneurs and any woman looking to achieve their version of success in business. Female Success Network attract women in business. Passionate, driven entrepreneurs, solopreneurs and women who have dreams and aspirations but need the clarity, strategy and clear goals to make their vision take shape.

Female Success Network was not using Pinterest. I was asked to take over and set up their Pinterest including their strategy. I completed the foundations of their profile, verifying their website, setting up rich pins and linking their website to Pinterest.

I also had to brainstorm what boards would be of interest, what keywords to use and what their ideal client was looking for on Pinterest.

We launched the site and created content that could be pinned daily. Where they didn't have original content we pinned other relevant content. We used the scheduler on Tailwind to ensure we pinned consistently and at our optimised times.

Female Success Network on Pinterest launched and they quickly started seeing massive growth in their engaged viewers and monthly viewers. They also had massive traffic going to their website. I wasn't responsible for conversion but what they were needing to do there was use opt-ins and generate leads for their email lists to build their following and convert clients to purchase.

Using Tailwind scheduling became fairly simple, we generated a pinning schedule and I devised the content strategy. I was given creative scope to create pins on Canva and schedule them in their website and on Pinterest.

The results were amazing. Quickly they saw monthly views at 500,000+ and an engaged audience of 100,00+. The traffic to their website was the highest from Pinterest too!

Here is what Sarah Stone Co-Founder of Female Success Network said about working with me.

Authors and Co

Authors and Co share their knowledge, expertise and process to help Female Entrepreneurs and Business Owners develop, write and market a book you have dreamed of writing and become an author. Authors and Co take a proven and unique approach to position women for the success and clients that you deserve.

Authors and Co were not using Pinterest and asked if I could set up their business account and using Tailwind create a pinning strategy. As with other profiles I set up their rich pins, verified their website and set up their profile. I completed the creation of all their pins using Canva.

Quite quickly they saw results of more traffic to their website and followers on Pinterest. Their monthly views are still at a few thousand each month.

Here is what Abigail Horne Co-Founder of Authors and Co said:

"Ally is your silent assassin working behind the scenes and getting amazing results! I used to think Pinterest was just looking at pretty things but I now know how important it is for your business. The conversion from Pinterest is massive and the traffic has increased to our website.

Ally always leads with honesty and integrity and is so much fun. I will always recommend Ally as the go to for Pinterest."

MY STORY

"**I**f it rains look for rainbows if its dark look for stars"

I have worked in a corporate career since the age of 19, you know where life just seems to fly by and before you know it 10 years of your life has gone. I have met some amazing people, my partner for one and my best friend, Sarah who at the age of 18 gave me my first Human Resources (HR) job!

At 19 I started my degree in Human Resources part time studying whilst working and graduated a few years later. You know I wasn't really what you would call academic. At school I despised maths but loved textiles, cooking and art.

I didn't think I would go on to complete a degree but that was probably one of my first big accomplishments I look back on now. It was tough working and studying at the same time.

When I was a little girl I was either going to be a singer or save the animals! To this day you will still find me with animals and singing in the shower!

At that time, I really enjoyed HR. Throughout my career I had worked my way up and across and had gone from role to role in various companies. I was adamant that I wanted to reach the top and become senior HR management by the age of 30. When I started out in my career that was always my goal, time stamped and if I didn't reach it by 30 I would have failed.

It's funny looking back now that I put so much pressure on myself to achieve this goal that in the end I believe that was my failing. Don't get me wrong, have goals, smash them, but make sure you have balance. Goals I believe need to be around your whole life and health and that's what I didn't appreciate at the time.

That goal it seemed was getting further and further away. There were changes in the company I was with and I was now in a purely recruiting role which wasn't really my passion. I started to reflect and really think about what I wanted, I really loved HR and the people aspect but there weren't options at that time to go back into the varied HR role. So, I started in Network Marketing.

I thought this would be a great focus for me and give me options for the future. I loved the company values and ethics and I saw a way to build my entrepreneurial side. The idea of building a team, supporting other's development and learning new skills was really exciting.

Then I became ill.

In October 2016, I had severe pains in my side that just seemed to get worse. I went to the doctors, was referred for scans and then late in November 2016 I was diagnosed with cancer. I say that so casually now but at the time it tore me and my family apart.

That day changed me forever.

I am very fortunate and grateful to say that it was actually a mis-diagnosis and it wasn't cancer. You see, four of my organs and my bones have lumps or lesions in them where my immune system has gone into overdrive, so on the original scans it looked like primary and secondary cancer.

It actually took five months and several biopsies to confirm that it definitely wasn't cancer. It was such an awful time waiting for the results of what it might be or could be. I wouldn't wish liver or spleen biopsies on anyone!! It was finally confirmed as a rare auto-immune disease called Sarcoidosis. What now...? I had never heard of such a thing!

At this point I have to say what an amazing family, friends and partner I have. They were my rocks throughout that time and I don't doubt that they found it incredibly difficult to always offer support and I appreciate them all.

I think it's fair to say after that, I probably did hit rock bottom, I didn't get out of my pyjamas for some time! I did wash and then put clean pyjamas on! I know this was a hard time for my family and especially Paul to watch.

I struggled and still struggle to manage the pain and fatigue and I think waiting five months of thinking it may be cancer, took such a toll on me mentally, while I was always trying to be strong for family's sake. I did celebrate my 30th Birthday in this time and had such an amazing time creating wonderful memories even given the circumstances.

I found it hard to focus on anything. I didn't feel I had any purpose, I wasn't at work, I didn't really feel like Ally, my life had changed and I had to get use to how my body felt. I felt weak, I can't do the things I use to do, I felt useless and just didn't know how to manage my pain and fatigue. I felt my relationships with my family had changed and nobody wanted to talk about the elephant in the room but I felt everyone was different with me.

I had a wonderful therapist who helped me see that this wasn't my fault and I didn't need to be defined by this. She gave me ways of managing my thoughts, pain and mindset. This is where I began my journey really investing time in the health of my mind and allowing myself time to grieve the old Ally.

You may be thinking I sound mad but to me I was never going to be that Ally again. Regardless of if I got better or not I had always been through this and that would have always changed me, so I had to grieve that person in a way and let go.

Techniques such as forgiving myself, writing, journaling and meditation were all of the ways I am able to sit here today and write my story. I can't emphasise enough if you take anything away from my journey please look after your health in mind and body.

I'm now 32 and I have accepted how I am and the path I am on. But I also have decided I will not be defined by my illness. Yes, some days I can't do very much, yes, some days the pain is worse, yes, some days I am exhausted but I am learning to manage this and accept this as part of my life.

I have always believed we have been put on this earth for a reason. We all have a purpose, that could be to make someone smile every day, it could be to be a mum, it could be to be a business woman. Either way I know I'm not done trying to find my purpose.

But I don't want people to know me as Ally who used to work in HR but is now ill, I want to be something more, I want to look forward to my future and be able to manage my life around my daily symptoms but ultimately create something of myself that I can be proud of and more than anything I want to make my family proud.

I always believed even when I was at school I would be more. I have so much to give this world and I'm not ready to give up now just because of a little bump in the road!

At that time apart from reading I spent a lot of time just aimlessly scrolling on Facebook! I am glad I did now because I came across the amazing Female Success Network. Divine timing or what? The beautiful ladies Abi and Sarah came into my life. To this day I will always be grateful to these two for how they have helped me get out of my pyjama world and get back in the real world!

Sarah and Abi were launching a free group for women who were looking for more success in their life and business. It struck a chord with me as I knew there was more to my life than to how it had become. I had no idea what I wanted to be when I grew up but I thought that they might help me progress a little further.

I joined the free Facebook group and instantly felt lifted. Sarah and Abi had put the Female Success Network together based around being heart centred and having your back. The group was engaging, supportive and inspiring.

I decided to book a call with Abi to discuss options to join the mastermind. Initially I thought it would help me focus again on what I could do with my Network Marketing business. I wasn't sure at this stage what my future would be with being able to go back to work and if I wanted that. Abi was so kind on that call and so understanding.

I instantly understood that they weren't there just for the money, they truly cared about the women they would be working one on one with and what success meant to them.

So, I joined the mastermind! I instantly felt like I had made a new bunch of friends. They were all so welcoming, supportive and inspiring. The mastermind provided me with focus to work on myself and achieve just one thing a day. In the beginning those things that I was achieving were small and very simple but the point being I celebrated achieving them with the mastermind.

Sarah and Abi have put structure in place so you can hold yourself accountable and reach out for support when you need it. I also got to have monthly strategy meetings with them. At the start we generally talked about me and what I liked and didn't and how I coped with my illness. They truly supported me by ensuring that I wasn't defined by that.

At the same time, low and behold to me they were slowly but surely pushing me into making decisions. Small decisions at first such as going for a walk, journaling, mediating, reviewing what I liked and didn't but all of it started making me take responsibility for my life and stop playing the victim.

They could see that I probably wouldn't go back to my old job and I wasn't going to be able to manage working for someone else. I was worried that I would let others down as I didn't know when I would have good days or bad days and I would hate to start have an awful attendance record.

So, they told me to go away and complete their target mastermind document. It helps you work through what your passionate about and what you are good at.

Back in School as I said I loved Art. Art was my favourite subject. I actually completed an A level in art and had all these dreams of travelling the world taking pictures and painting. At home I actually have a room full of paints, chalks etc. But life just got in the way and I hadn't got back into that.

I also love Pinterest. Pinterest to me is like a canvas with lots of beautiful images stuck on it and I think that's why I like it so much! It relates to my creative side. In the bad times Pinterest would be so easy to use, I would pin beautiful pictures of faraway places, or amazing photography. I would get lost in all those images and for a time it would take me away from where I actually was.

I really don't know how I ended up in HR, I always imagined myself in some worn out jeans and flipflops in some messy art room!

After completing this target mastermind word, I had a call with them both and they had asked if I had ever thought about having a business in Pinterest. They would probably look back at the call and laugh now at my face as I'm sure I looked so confused. I was really naïve to how you can basically set up a business in almost anything!

After that call, I went away and learnt everything I could about Pinterest. How to manage business accounts, the analytics, how to shop and sell on Pinterest, how to represent your brand on Pinterest however big or small, what the best pin is etc.

For most of this I was still in my pyjamas but the point being I had a focus each day, sometimes only a small one but it was so much more than I had before. And I was enjoying it, I love learning and felt I was unlocking a secret to this platform I had been using for ages.

Pinterest is like google, but it is a visual search engine. People often get confused that it's a social media platform but it's not. It's a search engine for visual discovery. You can use it to look for a recipe for dinner, a course on how to blog, beautiful photos or for questions to ask when on a date.

The options are endless! Pinterest works like little pin boards that you save all your ideas to. Do you remember when you use to cut and stick all your ideas to one piece of paper (usually out of the catalogues) well now you have Pinterest!

You can also shop direct from Pinterest, the latest fashion, documents and databases, home décor and so on. As you can tell I am a Pinterest Addict, there is so much variety and all genres are represented. I use this rather than google as I find looking at images far easier than text.

I have boards for my dream home, home décor,

inspiration, quotes, travel, photography and the list goes on.

Female Success Network was the first Pinterest account I worked on. I was super excited to implement what I had learnt and Sarah and Abi were so supportive, they just let me get on with it. I created pins, boards, and a content strategy and slowly we started to see the results.

Female Success Networks monthly views starting hitting near to 500k! I couldn't believe that the work I was putting in was actually getting results and good results! I was loving it! It was super exciting to see something I was doing actually having an effect.

The pin images were beautiful and the brand on Pinterest was just growing. I love working with this account because the brand is so beautiful and because it's about women. I get to create content, make the images and the pins and this takes me back to my love of art. Yes, it's online but I feel I have a creative edge that brings it all together.

I am really fortunate that I have been able to complete everything in the right steps because I have taken it at my pace and had such amazing guidance from the mastermind and Sarah and Abi.

If I needed to do some research I did it, if I needed to complete my business plan I did it, I didn't feel rushed or too overwhelmed at any point. Sarah and Abi let me take my time but pushed me when I needed pushing otherwise I think I may never have put myself out there! I don't doubt if I had not joined the mastermind I would not have been at this point at all. I know I wouldn't even have had the concept of starting a Pinterest Business.

If you are starting out on your business journey make sure you take it at your pace, but make sure there is a pace you have to get some things done even if it is just one thing. Also don't be rushed by anyone else and their timescales and have a plan of how you are going to launch a business and if there is a need for it!

I have only just recently launched so I won't be talking to you about how successful I am! This book is my first step, however I hope that in my first 12 months I can make a difference to peoples lives, by building their online presence and brand on Pinterest. I would also like to continue sharing my story and hope that it might inspire someone somewhere to seize the day and do what you love.

To be successful I do believe that you need certain habits and routine. My daily habits are around nourishing my body and mind, so all the usual drinking water, exercising, mediating and getting outside. Also making a weekly plan and staying organised. It's really important that you stick to your plan, that way you will feel more productive and that you have achieved something.

I also feel that to be successful you need to be loyal, lead with compassion and have integrity. I do everything I do with love, gratitude and integrity and I believe this will be my difference. Whatever stage of life you are in adopt some of these habits and I promise they will make a difference to your daily life and mindset.

Starting out I had the mastermind right behind me. Each of these women were so supportive. Some of my first clients were these women so I am forever grateful for their support and love. I have also created some educational courses for women who want to do Pinterest themselves.

My mission is to help as many Women as possible have a beautiful brand on Pinterest and help them be as successful as they can. I also am a Product Photographer which is another huge passion of mine. I wanted to incorporate photography without being tied to going out on shoots or having to meet clients on a specific date and time.

This enables me to complete photography in my own time and when feeling and giving my absolute best. I feel that both of these complement each other so well and I would never have pushed myself out there if Sarah hadn't seen the potential in me.

Success is a word that means so many different things to different people and that's what I love about the Female Success Network. It celebrates success in Life and Business. Success to me means having freedom to manage my illness, freedom to enjoy life, freedom to spend time with those I love, a business I am proud of and being the person that makes my family proud.

I feel right now I am working towards those things, we are never the final article we can always continue to learn and work on ourselves. I am a firm believer of the universe and of meditation and I don't think I would be where I am today if I hadn't invested time in to both of those. My family laugh at me when I say "don't put that out in the universe"! Only put love and positivity and that's what the universe will give you.

I am only just becoming a Female Entrepreneur. If I look back I have been through so much emotionally and mentally to get to this point, sometimes you really have to lean on yourself, give yourself a good talking to, pick yourself up and try again. I believe that deep down each and every one of us can be whatever we want to be.

Sometimes you need a little help from your friends and a good push. You have to stay true to your path and concentrate on your own journey. Don't get looking at what others are doing, receiving or achieving because they are not you. You must raise your energy and vibration and keep it high in order to walk your desired path.

You may be reading this and unsure if you want to start a business or not sure what in, then I would tell you this: Get support and surround yourself with Women who have your back, find a mentor, coach, cheerleaders, women you can go to in need of support and gentle coaxing and dare not to do it!

I always think especially on the bad days, what if I hadn't of started, what if I was too afraid not to make that jump, life is short and it must be lived to the best of our ability. I look back on this journey and I'm grateful for my illness because without it I wouldn't be where I am today.

I have met some incredible women with the help of Abi and Sarah have been able to design a business and life that I love. Life will always give you up's and down's that why it's called life but when it rains look for rainbows and when its dark look for stars.

ACKNOWLEDGMENTS

I have to start by firstly thanking Sarah Stone and Abigail Horne who have supported me from day one with this business idea. Sarah thank you for the amazing book cover and Abi through Authors and Co for publishing my book.

Thank you to all of my family for supporting my crazy ideas and for all your support with my illness. And thank you to Paul, my partner in crime and best friend for putting up with countless hospital visits, believing and taking a risk with me and a leap of faith that I could do this.

Notes

Information from https://business.pinterest.com/en-gb

Pinterest Accounts I have referenced:

https://www.pinterest.co.uk/kimberleybanner19/

https://www.pinterest.co.uk/sarahstoneonline/

https://www.pinterest.co.uk/authorsandco/

https://www.pinterest.co.uk/femalesuccessnetwork/

Join my community –

Pinterest @allydavis19

Facebook @allydavis190

Instagram ally_davis19

For information on my services visit
www.allydavis.com
For information about the course visit
www.getpintentional.com